MW01029316

Janice Gould carries us through the challenges and triumphs of her life with such carefully observed detail, such immediacy. At the end of one poem she writes about a woman she met when she was twenty-one, asking, *Hadn't she gazed steadily into my eyes?* And this is exactly what these poems do. By gazing steadily into one poet's experience, they show us the world.
— Ellen Bass, Judge of the Charlotte Mew Prize

Luminous with the tradition of Deep Song, or Cante Jondo, *The Force of Gratitude* is a journey through song and story of the love, longing, sorrow and beauty that shape a life. With a brave and intimate voice, each poem invites us into its "vibrant residence," into the rapturous landscapes of the heart.
— Jennifer Elise Foerster, author of *Leaving Tulsa*

Tracing the West coast from Berkeley to Portland to Vancouver, these poems and prose poems track a migratory youth. Pushed north, the speaker wanders, working as she goes: "I was the girl who bucked hay, split wood, tore the ragged face of earth with the harrow's teeth." But even as the young speaker moves from place to place, often in pursuit of elusive lovers, a profound sense of belonging also pervades these poems. Gould is at home in her own desire, at home in a natural world that is textured, sensory, endlessly arresting. When she describes the place where "mice skittered in milkweed, moles burrowed under stinging nettle," we live there too, and fall a little more in love with this world, this speaker, this poet.
— Jane Hilberry, author of *Still the Animals Enter* and *Body Painting* (Colorado Book Award for Poetry)

Vibrant love, passing cross country, is the salve of these poems. They are night sky constant, even in their journey into song. The journey is a transformation that trails light behind each wind, cloud, love, and vision from memory. Music is brought to language, language to music, but they remain together as one.
— Linda Hogan, award-winning Chickasaw author

The Force of Gratitude

Finalist for the Charlotte Mew Prize

The Force of
Gratitude

Janice Gould

Headmistress Press

Copyright © 2017 by Janice Gould
All rights reserved.

ISBN-13: 978-0997914948
ISBN-10: 0997914947

This book may not be reproduced, in whole or in part, including
illustrations, in any form (beyond that permitted by Sections 107
and 108 of the U.S. Copyright Law and except by reviewers for
the public press), without written permission from the publishers.

Cover art © 2016 Judy Chicago / Artists Rights Society (ARS), New York.
Judy Chicago, *Immolation: from the series Women and Smoke*

Cover & book design by Mary Meriam.

PUBLISHER
Headmistress Press
60 Shipview Lane
Sequim, WA 98382
Telephone: 917-428-8312
Email: headmistresspress@gmail.com
Website: headmistresspress.blogspot.com

For Mimi

Contents

This Music

Why this longing, this desire to sing sadness
or adoration? In some dark layer music forms,
note upon note, phrase after phrase, each cadence

bearing the blue of sky, thickness of clouds piled
at the horizon, a flight of birds pushed by relentless wind.
Melody is borne in snowmelt and flood, in the rock cliff's edge,

in the leap of fire across a chasm. Rhapsody reflects
the shine of mica, glint of sunlight in aspen, a tree's long shadow.
Each aria seeks to find you close to me, open to rapture.

Gacela of First or Second Love

Hoping to see her after school,
I would wait at the stop
for the Number Seven at Milvia
and University, the bus she took too.
Choosing the seat behind her
or just across, I'd wish she would
turn her head, notice me.

To sit near her, observe her calm
hands holding a book while
the lumbering vehicle made its way
past Northgate and up Euclid
to Rose Walk with its Maybeck houses
—how devious. Sometimes

I would stare beyond her profile,
past Berkeley's twisting streets
and narrow paths, feeling leavened
when strands of her light hair
fell along her cheek as she
inclined her head to read.

I ached to say something to her—
mariposa, marigold, marry me!—
but never could. At the next stop
she would step down into a world
of Plane trees and neat gardens,
into a family, so normal,
so unlike mine,
I could hardly breathe.

The Girl I Used to Be

I was the girl who backed into life,
got lost, then disappeared again
under tables and in drawers,
between unused tools hung
on dusty pegs, among red lines
etched on imaginary maps.
In Spring I watched waxwings sway
drunkenly among sour berries
and found myself pushed north with them
in torn clouds, landing where rhododendrons grow
on wet hillsides, and larkspur pokes
from granite, waving small blue flags.

I was the girl who bucked hay, split wood,
tore the ragged face of earth with the harrow's teeth,
who tried to toughen up in leather boots and haying chaps,
became invisible in snow or rain,
beat her fists on windshields, but
survived by singing late into the night,
driving deserted streets
while everyone else was wasted.

I was the girl who seldom spoke,
who slept alone fully clothed, ready to bolt
into the startled dawn. Then one day
enticed by stones, this girl plunged into
a clear Sierra stream and rose, gasping
from that brutal creek, terrified,
but absolutely clean.

Thumbing to Tacoma

The police picked us up as soon as we stepped off the I-5 Bridge, having just crossed the Columbia River. Both eighteen, we had decided to hitch a ride to her hometown. The officer ushered us into his black-and-white and took us to the police station, a small brick building in Vancouver. I carried my steel-string Martin guitar and some clothes in a borrowed airlines bag: underwear and socks, a clean shirt, a Navy blue pullover, my toothbrush. After my girlfriend called home, her dad wired money, and before long an officer was escorting us to the bus depot in a squad car. *You girls know hitching is dangerous, not to mention illegal in the state of Washington?* Illegal? Really? We pleaded ignorance and caught the local Greyhound north to Tacoma.

The bus pulled off the Interstate at all the small towns—Kelso, Centralia, Lacey, and detoured into Fort Lewis, where a few soldiers boarded and stared at us with hard, hungry eyes. My sweetheart, who had surreptitiously put her arm through mine and sat close as we passed through the wintry countryside, now pulled away but kept her knee pressed against mine. The trip through the base seemed long and slow. Those boys with shaved heads would ship out to Vietnam soon, but that was no concern of mine. I was against the war, sure, weren't we all? I came from Berkeley. We Berkeley people hated the war. I came of age singing songs like Buffy St.-Marie's "Universal Soldier." I didn't know any military guys, but I didn't think anyone should go fight wars.

Her dad met us at the station, where he gave his daughter a hug and tipped his cap to me, smiling. When we got into his white Volkswagen, there were no scolds or reprimands. Father and daughter seemed comfortable together. They laughed and joked. He admired the parka she was wearing—she showed him the Velcro cuffs, the heavy zipper, and admitted she had borrowed it from me. "I want one just like it," she said.

They lived on a hill, in a condo. Her dad was an organist at one of the universities, must have taught music. Her mom was a housewife. A slender little lady with thin, permed hair, she seemed dubious about me, dressed as I was, so boyish. Maybe she didn't like Indians. I had met people who felt that way. But my girlfriend's father took to me, asked me questions. I played guitar for them. Later, they let us sleep in the same room, in the same bed, and she, disrobed, was lithe, with long brown hair and tan skin, coloring from her dad.

In the morning, while it snowed lightly, we sat with her father in the dining room and talked. I was amused by his breakfast, which was like my own father's—a soft-boiled egg, wheat toast with marmalade, and orange juice mixed with cranberry. He made coffee in an Italian pot I had brought my girlfriend as a gift when I came north—and which she had sent to her father, saying he would love such a device. He thanked me now as the little pot steamed and whistled. His eyes sparkled with appreciation when he poured Espresso into our cups. I glanced at my lover, who sat across from me at the table. Did her father know what a fervent tenderness I harbored for his daughter? Like my dad, her father stirred sugar into his coffee—one spoonful, two—and added Half and Half. He was humming a tune. Was it Bach? He stirred, sipped. *Ahh,* he said, and smiled. Would he hate me if he knew?

Song

I'm driving to Steilacoom
in the blue VW bug
I bought with my cannery wages.
I'm driving there because
you told me you like that word.
Steilacoom, Steilacoom,
you would say. Not much
in that Indian place,
but I'm driving north
because you might be there,
standing by the tracks, contemplating
the water that laps against the cold shore.
Because winter is a desperate time—too much
rain, too much snow—and friendless—
too many shadows, too much alone.
Maybe in Steilacoom we will embrace.
Perhaps there you will take my hand,
forgive my inconsistencies,
sit with me till a sudden sun
pours down its light,
brightening Puget Sound, offering
a far view of mountains,
beckoning and proud. Beyond that
I want nothing. Only to see you
in Steilacoom, Steilacoom,
only to find you
in that town.

Coming Up Short

I sat sweating in the warm office
of a man in white shirt and fat tie
while he slurped coffee
and pored over my application.
Trying to look eager for a job,
I had borrowed my friend's dark skirt from Spain,
wore a matching suede jacket,
a pair of plain brown loafers, no socks.
A January torrent had blown against my body,
my shoes squished with rainwater,
my feet felt cold and numb.
I had no training for anything—
could play guitar, oboe, but had acquired
no skills to help me join
the world of labor.

They tested me, found I had nimble fingers.
I could fit tiny brass washers and screws
to transistor radios if I were at least
five feet, two inches tall.
I wasn't.

We'll call if anything comes up.

In my wallet were three dollars
and a check for thirty that a bank manager
refused to cash when she decided
I had forged my aunt's signature.
The lady had not even said, *I'm sorry,*
but had regarded me coldly, unsmiling.
She stood up from her desk to indicate
I should leave.

At the Employment Office, my legs itched.
I hoped the man had not noticed
the small leaves and bits of dirt
that had splashed on my ankles and calves.
I felt like a fool, holding back tears
that soon washed away in the rain.

Poor in Spirit

You, at midnight, suddenly awake,
blinking in the yellow light
of the single bulb
hanging from the ceiling.
You, in a disheveled nightgown,
pushing back your brown hair,
coughing, smiling shyly at me.
You, coming to my bed
not many nights later,
gazing into my eyes,
saying little, your finger tracing
my mouth. You leaning on
the shoulder of your boyfriend,
his arm around your waist. You
still watching me. You
with your nervous laugh,
your jumpiness, your
too-many-drugs.
You locked-down
in an overheated psych ward,
hunched over,
hugging yourself,
not looking at me,
while outside,
beyond wire-meshed windows,
Portland traffic stalled and started
along the old highway, a train
hooted at a nearby crossing,
guys in business suits spanked
young go-go girls in smoky clubs,
and a murder of crows mocked and scolded
among the downed leaves of winter trees.

Au Revoir

The Greyhound Bus chuffed through the Willamette Valley, stopping at each burg along the way—Corvallis, Woodburn, Beaverton. Snow descended on and off, alighting on fir trees, frozen ponds, leafless oaks and maples. Arriving in Portland just before nightfall—it was the first day of a new year—a caravan of buses groaned and rumbled in the chilly air. Crowds of people milled about, talking, smoking, smelling of sweat, perfume, wet wool. In the cavernous echo of the terminal a nasal voice called out the next arrival and departure on the scratchy PA, and a moment later I spotted you striding through the depot in your faux leopard-skin coat, your wavy hair crimped under a black beret. You saw me, waved, rushed up to give an awkward hug, saying, *"Ça va, chèrie?"* Laughing, we pushed our way out the heavy, double-paned glass doors into the winter damp.

The streetlight decorations—holly and bells, poinsettias and candy canes—gave the city a festive air, though they appeared bedraggled after the wind and snow of a Pacific storm. You hailed a Yellow Cab and we clambered in—my first taxi ever—slipping through city streets, over the Burnside Bridge. I could see the Willamette River, cold and steely, encased between concrete flood walls, wooden wharves, and other bridges—Hawthorne, Morrison, Broadway—dotted with lights, heavy with traffic. You lit a *Gauloise* and hummed a little tune, cracking the window slightly to exhale the smoke.

Although not much older than me, you seemed world-weary. Nothing surprised you. After high school you had traveled with a girlfriend in Europe, could speak passable French, loved Piaf and Brel. We listened to them that evening, disparaging our former dorm life in the provincial town where we had attended college, me for one semester, you for a year. I had admired your red hair and milky skin, your sighs of boredom or exasperation when in the presence of nattering co-eds. You had seemed brave in your non-conformity and independence.

That night, patting your barely rounded belly, you revealed that you were four months pregnant, and shared that you could not go to your motherless home in Tacoma, could not tell your widowed father. He would beat you. No man was currently in the picture, no lover who called for you. There was also no doctor, no medical help, little food. Occasionally there was marijuana or hashish, opium or LSD, brought by an acquaintance, bought on the street. I volunteered to stay, which seemed to please you. Weeks later, unable to find a job, even at minimum wage, my money ran out. Helpless, no longer useful, I returned to California.

One day, unexpectedly, you called me—you were in Berkeley. Three or more years had passed. Invited to meet you in a house south of campus, a Victorian on Derby or Carleton, I drove down in the old Chevy pickup my dad was letting me drive. It was near twilight, and I suggested we take a spin in the hills to get a view of the bay. You still walked with long, swaying strides, still smoked cigarettes—but now they were mentholated Newports. Climbing into the Chevy's cab, you shrugged off your black leather coat, revealing a dusky pink sweater and dark gabardine skirt. I wanted to tell you about my studies, my writing—I had finally gone back to school—but you said you hadn't much time. Our talk was stilted, punctuated by silence, and though I hadn't thought to ask, you informed me that you'd given up the baby for adoption. I headed back to your neighborhood, and you gestured for me to park behind a long black sedan. "My pimp's car," you smirked. When I said nothing, you started laughing. Before slamming the truck's door, you jeered, "You're such a *naïf!* This whole time with you I've been on smack, flying high as a bat!"

Crazy Twenty-One

It took no time for my boots to wear out as I walked around the hay field following my boss, who worked the finicky baler that, when it behaved, swept up the windrows and spit out rectangular bales held together by string. Using hay hooks, I hoisted the bundles of cut oats into stacks four high and two deep, each layer crossways to the other. I liked the work, but by noon my feet ached, my shirt was soaked with sweat.

At lunchtime we sat in the tall grass by the side of a dirt road eating sweet pickles with egg salad sandwiches on home-baked bread, and swigging cold lemonade brought to us by the boss's pretty wife who, baby in tow, spent the hour with us. Thin, crisp molasses cookies were dessert, and then deep draughts of cold water out of a thermos, fresh from the spring.

When we finished eating, it was back to work. Sun shone overhead, blue sky throbbed, and a stray cloud wandered east on the afternoon breeze. At the edge of the field stood a forest of oaks, Douglas fir, and vine maples, a thick screen of shadowy undergrowth. Along the creek, redwing blackbirds chattered among the cattails. It was perfect—even though she had driven back to the ranch, their baby buckled into his car seat, a dust cloud trailing her vehicle. Because wasn't her smile, when she looked at me, gentle and genuine? Hadn't she gazed steadily into my eyes?

Library

Our crew of women huddled around the electric heater, sipping coffee before starting work. Outside, the earth was wet and cold from a January thaw, but I knew snow was coming, could smell it on the morning breeze. After awhile our supervisor, Betty, sent Mary and me upstairs into the loft where fifty-pound bags of cedar chips—used for smoking game and fish—were stored. We emptied several bags of wood chips into an enormous hopper, and when that was done, I stood in the open, barn-like doorway looking out at the trees on this wooded edge of town, and at the muddy parking lot. Shannon, late for work, was backing her black, 1939 Ford Coupe next to my blue VW bug. Minutes later, after being barked at by Betty for tardiness, Shannon was standing next to me in the assembly line, gluing down the top flap on boxes of wood chips. "I brought you some commodities," she told me. "Gosh," I said, "you didn't have to do that. I've got food." "Well," she answered, "we had more than we needed. It's just a little box—peanut butter, a can of lard, some rice and whatnot. Really, we had plenty." I smiled at her. "Thank you. That's really kind." Shannon didn't say anything, just grinned back.

I knew she had four children to feed, that her husband didn't make much more than she did. They were from Oklahoma—"Okies," one of my co-workers sneered. During the warm months in California, to which they would soon return, they picked pears, plums, almonds, and grapes. But now, in Oregon, they had found factory work and a house to rent only a few blocks from downtown Hood River. They invited me for Christmas— sharing their roast turkey and macaroni salad, along with potato chips (my contribution), soda pop for the kids, and a half case of beer for the adults. A couple of store-bought apple pies sat on a counter—the dessert. I hadn't been there long before Shannon and her husband Ralph, taking advantage of the holiday, excused themselves and disappeared into their bedroom, where Charley Pride was belting out "Kaw-liga" on the stereo. While the adults were busy, their teen-aged daughter Kelly invited me to see the "library" in an upstairs room she shared with her sister.

Her library was a long shelf of dilapidated paperbacks that included titles like *Jane Eyre, The Brothers Karamazov, Catch-22,* as well as a sizable number of Louis L'Amour. "You've read all these books?" I asked Kelly, trying not to look surprised. "Oh, yes," she said. "But where do you find them?" "Thrift stores. Goodwill." she replied, nonchalant. "I see," I said, but I didn't see. I had never been in a thrift store or a Goodwill. I was either always provided for, or I earned enough that I went to a bookstore for my books, to a department store for my clothes. I didn't know you could find "classics" at Goodwill. I didn't know what you could find. "I want to be a librarian when I grow up," Kelly told me. I nodded, looking at her collection, which I saw was organized by the author's last name. I suddenly felt a sweet, sad affection for this girl. I looked at her face while she gazed proudly at her books. I didn't know if her parents were literate, didn't know how much schooling either of them had. It occurred to me that Kelly would not find a permanent home while her parents moved from place to place, the '39 Coupe and the '50s pickup truck loaded with all their earthly possessions—pots, pans, blankets, clothes, and a few boxes of tattered but well-read books.

Luhr's Lures

The women called Luhr Jensen's shop Luhr's Lures, the place we assembled ovens for smoking fish, where lures were also made. My job in January was to fill boxes with cedar chips in a warehouse at the edge of town, but in February I was transferred to the main shop downtown and taught to bend pieces of aluminum for the electric ovens. Some days I soldered together small grills, added wiring to these contraptions. It was fun working with the gaggle of women who hollered to each other across the shop, laughing and gossiping. After I discovered a stash of gin hidden in a cabinet beneath the sink, a woman who was cozy with the foreman told him I had taken some nips from the bottle—I hadn't—so I was transferred to a building up the street where I worked alone for eight hours, gluing together little cardboard cartons for the fancy lures.

The job was intolerable. The following week I quit. It was March by then. My friends Steve and Martha, who lived in a dinky trailer in Husum, would sometimes let me stay with them. I slept on their loveseat sofa, and in the morning took a quick shower, ate a bowl of cold cereal, and then Steve drove us to Luhr's in his old two-tone Studebaker. He was an ex-logger, a liberal, and an excellent woodcarver, but his prize possession was a Gibson hollow body, electric guitar that he played with a country swing. He had married hunchbacked Martha, a warm-hearted woman with a twisted face, who was the twin sister of lovely Mary, with whom I worked and with whom I was infatuated. But by Valentine's Day Mary had moved back to Portland, reunited with her children and husband, Dave, a lanky biker. I lived with them for a while, too, in that lull of northwest Spring weather when it doesn't rain for a couple of weeks. Without work, I knew I would soon wear out my welcome, and so it happened. Dave listened to the engine of my car one evening, pronounced it good to go, loaned me twenty dollars, and I rolled out of town just as the weather changed and a snowstorm blew down out of Washington state. It followed me all the way to the Oregon border, and I spent a freezing night in a highway Rest Area by the Klamath River in the backseat of my VW bug, encased in a nylon sleeping bag, sleek and somnolent as a trout.

Prodigal

The door was locked when I got home to Berkeley and I had no key, no idea when anyone would show up. I got my sleeping bag from the car, the brown nylon I had picked up at the Sporting Goods store in Hood River, and because it was March and chilly, put it down on the chaise lounge on the verandah, took off my boots, and climbed in. I had been gone a year, had not come home for holidays, had not written, seldom called, wasn't sure I wanted to be home, but I had no other place to go.

I was dozing when I heard Mom drive her Mustang into the carport. Not sure how I would be greeted, my heart raced. I thought about pretending to be asleep, but knew I wouldn't be able to pull it off. I heard the trunk slam shut, two voices—my younger sister was with Mom. Their footsteps scuffed the concrete stairs, and I heard my sister say, "There's someone on the porch." I sat up, disentangled myself from the sleeping bag, and stood looking over the rail of the verandah. Mom had stopped midway up the stairs, and when she saw me, scowled. "So. You've come home." She resumed climbing. When she reached the top of the stairs, she walked across the porch to the front door, juggled the grocery bag to her left arm, and inserted a key in the deadbolt. She pushed open the door and went in. My sister, following, paused and looked at me, and before going inside, shrugged her shoulders, shook her head. I sighed, pulled on my boots, and, to gain a bit of time, rolled my sleeping bag but left it on the chaise.

"I expect you want to live here again," Mom said, pulling cans of soup out of the shopping bag without looking at me. We were standing in the kitchen. "Yes," I replied, "if I can." "Well. And what are you going to do? Get a job?" "If I can." "If you can," she answered. Her lips were pursed. "Doing what?" "I don't know." She looked at me, her face hard. "You don't know." I looked down at my boots and said nothing. Those Tony Lamas had cost me a week's wages. I bought them the past summer, working on the ranch. They were sturdy leather, had steel reinforced toes. I had worn them day after day for seven months. They were scraped, but in good shape. "Oh, for God's sake," she muttered, and walked out of the room.

Gacela of September Dawn

Your throat, dear one, was the target
of my kisses those September dawns
when we were in our twenties.

At night we watched stars shift
across the sky, talked among tangled sheets,
our clothes strewn on the floor.

Crickets sang beneath the window,
mice skittered in milkweed,
moles burrowed under stinging nettle.

At dawn, mourning doves courted
in the eucalyptus and autumn drifted
like a faint insinuation from the foothills,

where fires had begun to burn. When you took
another lover, sat in his lap, kissed him
while I watched, laughed at my confusion

and pain, I blazed with cold hatred,
ground you to zero in my mind.
I ached to slap your lovely face.

Winter Gacela

Had I been stronger, truer,
we might have gone together,
you huddled against me
in the cab of my pickup.
I would drive to the foothills
under leafless orchards,
negotiating the two-lane roads
with one hand clutching yours,
passing open, muddy fields,
moody tangles of blackberries,
thickets of poison oak. Our breaths
misting the truck's windows,
we would gaze through the season's
freezing fog, notice a blue heron rise
from a patch of marshland.
We could hear the shrill cries of snow geese
as they hunkered down for the damp months
among California's reeds and ricelands—
where rats and voles multiply, and feral cats
prowl in the black soil of memory.

Gacela of Bamboo and Plum Blossoms

We are living in a Hiroshige woodcut,
weathered houses with blue tile roofs,
bamboo gates, gardens of azaleas,
jasmine, and tea roses, delicate and spicy.
Amid these sits a stone Buddha, placid
with inward gazing.

"There is more than one path
to the top of the mountain,"
you assure me while a flock of blackbirds
alights in scraggly pines.

On the bay a few small boats tilt
among whitecaps, sails open
in the fulsome wind. Across the water
the peak gleams, mantled with redwoods
and spruce, while the ocean laps
at the long stretch of pebbled beaches.

The piping whales are rolling,
diving on their great migrations,
waving fins at gawking tourists
who huddle on cliffs among parsnips and thistles.

Here, on the steep, winding streets of our city
plum trees blossom, pink and passionate
with crooked boughs that smell like imported baskets,
like dyed cloth and paper, like damp gardens.

Far off a mist suddenly thickens,
clouds churn up, and whistling rain rushes in,
pouring down—pushing me into the next panel.

Stumbling, sullen, bent, bedraggled,
I pull my coat close and look to find you.
Alas, you have fallen in with the rabble.
Over the arched bridge you dance,
damp and jostled—disappearing
in a procession of gongs and drums.

Laura: One

She stood by the window in her apartment on Durant, looking out at the dark street, where cars swished by in the rain. The place smelled of rice and *chiltoma* cooking on the stove, of strong coffee and cigarettes. No more than fourteen years old, but already married, she turned and glanced at me, where I sat in a chair by the table, then turned back to the window. She tapped her foot. She was humming a Nicaraguan tune in her husky voice while I found chords for them on my guitar. Her black hair fell past her shoulders. I got up and stood behind her, put my arms around her waist. In all the weeks of knowing her, I had never touched her, though I had often wanted to. Now she relaxed into me and swayed a little, as if dancing a slow *mambo* or *merengue*. We stood that way tenderly. Her hair was fragrant. I pushed it aside to kiss the back of her neck, but she swiveled around, facing me. Putting her arms around my neck, she looked into my eyes. Her eyes were brown like the darkest chocolate, her lashes thick and black, her teeth as she smiled very white, small, and even. She kissed me, next to my mouth, then moved quickly away just as the sound of her husband's key turned the lock in the door. I leaned toward the windowsill, caught my breath, and turned to say *hola* to the handsome young man who had brought her to this country. My heart was racing. What we had just done was like a dream; she had wanted me to hold her. I was flushed with disbelief, and the brief warmth of her against me. Later, I wondered if she had seen him coming, if she was aware that he would, at any moment, be at their door, the very instant she kissed me.

Your Beauty

When I first saw you in the university halls,
among graduates and undergraduates,
a tremor seized me, and I cursed

under my breath, thinking, "Yes, it's her."
You came to me, asked if I had the time. I should have
said, looking into your eyes, "For you,

I will always have time." We might have laughed.
Later our flirtation filled, but emptied me too—
the embrace, the kiss at the crown of my head,

the shy conversations. Your intensity
could blaze, you of quick and lovely insights.
I burned in fierce desire. What could I

give you? I wanted to take you
by the waist, kiss your throat, and feel
beneath my fingers your thin back. I wanted

to praise you, dreamed of being your first,
best lover. Your beauty tears me still,
your eager concerns, the range of your good mind,

your silences, things you never said. But now
I remember how you once stood before me, your body
trembling, the steel in your eyes hardening—

for I had wickedly displeased you.

Look Back

Driving east along the Interstate, you looked back
and saw me standing at the edge of the lava cliffs,
contemplating the river.
Yes, I was there in my Levis and torn shirt,
my hair disheveled by the wind, skin
turned brown beneath the sun.

The smell of tarweed rose from hot soil,
from the nearby pines
the scent of pinesap.

It was thirty years ago or more,
but I was filling up on wonder
and longing.

The big river churned far below,
the water coursing down from Canada,
the distant Rockies.

I wanted even then your sweetness,
your hands reaching across the table
to grasp mine.

I wanted you to look back,
to tell me later how you knew
it was me you saw waving,

my fingers tracing an arc against the sky.
How it made you smile,
my signaling so ardently.

Elegy

I.

In that wing of the hospital other families confer. We must look the same—dazed and inward. In her room, our father in a pale nightgown, seems asleep, attached as she is to machines. I watch while my older sister works lotion into our father's feet and hands, speaking in the voice she uses when she gentles one of her horses.

My younger sister tells us she noticed an orderly treating Dad roughly, calling Barbara "him," disdainful of our father's transgendered body, the male figure reshaped into a feminine form. One of my sisters has brushed Barbara's sparse white hair. Pink skin at the crown of her head, the blue veins of her eyelids.

Days ago, snow fell on the highest slopes of Mt. Diablo. It persists. Meanwhile on the lush foothills wild mustard waves a brazen flag in Spring wind, poppies open their luminous cups.

II.

Two Spirits they are called today, but in traditional times they were called by their tribal names, *Nadleehi, Koshkalaka, Hwame,* lyrical words that recognized the phenomenon of men the spirit had transformed into women, women the spirit altered into men. A great power dictated this arrangement, allowing distinct humans to walk between and among the single-gendered people, those who comfortably performed their assigned roles and duties, who felt no proclivity to take up an opposite identity. Two Spirits sometimes married people of the same sex and made excellent partners, knowing how to please others, how to be the other, how to be themselves. No fear, no shame. It is said that if one's fate is determined by power, one must follow its directive, and can no more go against it than one can go against gravity. Thus we learn and remember: we are as much spirit as flesh.

III.

After our dad had passed, my sisters and I walked in the hills south of Moraga, where, late in the nineteenth-century or early in the twentieth, farmers planted fruit and nut trees: pears, apples, walnuts, and almonds. People owned little vacation homes in Orinda, Rheem, and Lafayette, and travelled by rail to these villages on weekends from Berkeley and Oakland. The vestiges of those groves still stand, flowering in the Springtime.

The wind had come up that day and was rippling the tall oat grass. Clouds scudded by as shafts of sunlight brightened that green world, warmed our faces if we looked up and closed our eyes. No one talked much till, below the crest of a hill, we noticed, next to a patch of milkweed, the straight up plume of a skunk's tail. Someone yelled and we ran for it, collaring the dogs as we went, leaping over milkweed and thistles, avoiding rabbit holes, scrambling as far down the hill as we could get before starting to laugh at our quick dash, our panic, our near miss.

And then there we were, three sisters, under canyon oaks and laurels, watching a pair of Western bluebirds flit from fencepost to fencepost. The day was waning. Night would come in a few hours—it being February, time of snow or of sudden blossoming. We had bid farewell to both our dear parents, would eventually scatter their ashes. One of us would be next, leaving the others behind. But for now we were together—grateful, grieving—each reverent in her own way.

Holy Wind

The Navajo say wind enters us at birth, and when we die
it spirals up and out through the tops of our heads,
the whorls of fingers and toes.

Each spring, wind brings its shadows and troubles,
slitting wide the sky, whipping topsoil into clouds of dust,
corkscrews of red grit.

In summer, wind storms down canyons,
veers off rocks, shears snow from the face of mountains
shaking fire from the sky.

Wind nudges unfurled leaves and discourages sparrows
who perch tenacious amid tossing branches.
Rattling panes of glass at night, wind

flutes through cracks and under sills
while stars whirl through the dark depths,
heedless and distant. When sunrise shimmers

at the edge of the mesa, we wake to roads swept hard,
raked to a stony surface, and breathe
a common breath. Wind is relative to each of us—

animals, insects, earth, you and me.
It seems we are nothing but a vibrant residence
sheltering that cadenced force, that vast sigh.

Lavanda que te quiero lavanda

After Federico García Lorca

Lavender, how I love you lavender,
violet eyes, indigo lashes,
mountains at dawn, rivers at sunset.
Lavender, how I want you lavender:
scent of lilac on your neck,
floral hint of wine we sip,
your flashes of wit, sweet, dark,
tender, like shadows on snow,
like broken branches. Beguiling
like a girl, your body a meadow
where daylight lingers into long hours,
and twilight is somber, quiet,
and pensive as stars appear slowly
in a deep purple sky. *Ausencias y nostalgia,*
la triste música del tango, fog in November
on the streets of San Francisco,
smell of baked bread and black coffee,
taste of pastilles, lavender stones
and penumbra. Your beautiful mouth
in a bruising month of winter.

Conditions for Poetry

It should be dark—not absolutely,
but opalescent as dawn
in the hour before sunrise,
or the blue-gray of evening
as twilight gathers over the mountain.
The air should be chilly
and the only sound the small,
mechanical heartbeat of a clock
in another room.
If it is morning, coffee is called for,
oily, aromatic; if evening, a glass of red wine,
translucent, smelling of cherries.
Preferably it is Friday with rain
pattering the window,
Bachianas Brasileiras pouring
from an old radio
in a mahogany cabinet—
and we are in Berkeley or Berlin.
If Berkeley, the rain smells of the sea,
or of laurel and redwood.
If Berlin, the air is rank
with cigarettes and traffic.
Branches of linden trees shudder in the wind.
A presence stands just beyond
the closed door to your room,
attentive, listening. Or perhaps
not listening, not there,
not even thinking of you:
austere in her own life,
busy and elegant as tapestry,
fantastic as a fugue.

The Crags

For Suzanne MacAulay

We made our way in late afternoon
up the slope above the cold creek.
Rain had swept through not an hour before,
but the red earth seemed already dry
except in high meadows. There,
beneath willows, black mud glistened,
fertile and radiant, and an occasional sparrow
flitted, elusive. Ahead of me, you disappeared
around a curve, sprightly walker,
quick as a wren. I lagged behind,
marveling at your speed and endurance
as I slowed on each gravelly incline,
breathing hard.

Tall spruce were quiet, thick with foliage,
and the aspens' leaves flickered, late summer green.
In granite crevices I noticed patches of moss
dotted with twigs and pine needles, sometimes
breathed the fragrance of sap. In the meadows,
we came upon asters, harebell, thick-stemmed gentian.
Meanwhile a flotilla of clouds crossed the sky,
streaming their banners.

The wind at the crags was cold, buffeting us
where we sat among ocher rocks.
Suddenly a gust pushed back your hair
revealing a blue vein in your forehead
and the shape of your skull,
vulnerable and dear.
But you were smiling,
exhilarated, perched on the stone outcrop
and the earth that bears us—
sun-lit and self-contained.

Sometimes I Imagine

She arrived at my door early, saying, *It was the maze of streets, I couldn't find my way to the Chancellor's and gave up.* Stepping into my apartment's narrow hall, she looked fragile and harried. *I hope you don't mind,* she said. Only a day or two before she had learned about the cancer growing in her daughter's breast.

In our new friendship, we had hiked where old ranchland gives way to a military base—could hear sometimes the muffled throb of artillery—had walked the meander of trails, spotting Western Bluebirds, Say's Phoebes, goldfinches, towhees, a Prairie Falcon. In the meadows among Gambel's oaks, we listened to the wing-trills of hummingbirds and watched the hover and swoop of a Rufous, who circled high in a looping arc. On an upper ridge, in a belt of ponderosa, warblers said, *tcheck, tcheck, tcheck.*

She perched at the edge of the sofa, sipped from her glass, and said little, looking stunned. Sometimes I imagine how I could have walked over, pulled her to her feet (she would have said, *Oh! What?*), and put my arms around her. How could we know then that her daughter's health would return, her body bearing a grandchild?

****

During the last summer of my mother's life when the tumor had filled her belly, I sometimes left her for a day, driving up the coast those August afternoons, and walking worn tracks and deer paths along the headland while a bank of fog shrouded the ocean west of the Farallon Islands. Damp smell of alders along the creek, warm smell of fescue and oat grass in the upslope of meadows where cow parsnips bobbed in the wind that fluttered and twisted their petals. Misty air over the bay and *estero,* scrub jays calling, a Snowy Egret winging slowly over a marsh.

I was obscurely angry with my mother for needing me, but probably I was her closest friend, and the only one who saw her sobbing one night when she realized her life would come to an end sooner than any of us expected. I remember waking after midnight to the sound of weeping, and got up to find Mom in her nightgown, seated on the stairs, face in hands. She was crying furiously. *Oh, God...*she said. *I'm going to die!* I backed away.

Sometimes I imagine sitting down beside my mother and putting my arms around her. I would hold her tightly, and let her weep into my body, absorbing her salt, her fear and grief, her loneliness.

One Star

One star gleams above the dark edge of the mountains,
one star or one planet, bright with reflected light.

One moon shines down on the valley west of here,
floating in hazy clouds. One bird calls from the *piñón,*

only one, and one mountain, far south, snow on its flanks,
grows distinct in the dusky glimmer before dawn. I wish

I had tobacco and sweet grass to make an offering to the night,
to give myself fully to prayer, to reside in the song of that bird.

I want to be without words, without speech, to find my way
into a language so fine it becomes nothing but melody.

Desde mi casita

Awake at two a.m., a winter in Santa Fe.
Outside, the streets pile with ice and snow,
junipers hunker against fierce wind.
Silence of adobes, glitter of stars.

Cante jondo

Wind taps the window at night,
whistles through cracks and keyholes,
summoning. Along the snowy ridge
she moans a black *siguiriya*.

I work as darkness encloses my house,
sleep dreamlessly in the afternoon.
When I awaken, burning and hungry,
I listen for wind. She'll come

scratching holes in sandy soil,
kicking up gravel, sobbing and singing,
the train of her dark skirt
swaggering magnificently.

What Dawn Brings

A solitary raven wings from the *piñón*
as sky lightens to azure.

Sun warms the kitchen counter and a few ants
venture forth, exploring.

I watch, sipping coffee, intrigued by their industry,
their single-minded purpose.

I wander from room to room, stare out the glass doors,
write a few lines—feeling my way

through stone and mud like the root of a tree,
the smallest tendril

scratching millimeter by millimeter to secure
a place in the world.

Mad Girl's Gacela

You cannot touch her craziness,
though you wish to try.
Try eating dirt from the chapel at Chimayó,
holding hot wax in your hands,
or skating on a pond of holy water.
Try climbing atop the altar to kiss
the lips of a fastidious saint
chiseled from a club of cottonwood.
Loll with the worms that emerge from the dog
curled by the side of the road. Be silent
as the marrow of old bones,
the dust on the window sill.
Walk barefoot in December
along the creek's frozen bed,
among branches and thorns,
where stones whisper back
when you tell them your secrets.

Try biting a cactus, a crocus,
a wild rose, while chittering at birds
who cross their eyes at you.
Read from the bible of sooty rocks
rooted in poisonous soil.
Then inhabit the husky shouts
of that girl raging at the burst walls
of her house, its broken mirrors
and stained floors, scorched pots
and rusted pans.
Feast on her tears,
the crepuscular sky of her shames,
her shivering hormones.
Tangle your fists in her hair
and accept her slaps and scratches,
the way she pounds on your heart—
keep back. Keep Back!

Violence

A morning in late spring, before sun-up, the cat chasing moths at the kitchen window—Miller moths that migrate in from the plains on their way to the mountains. They'll take advantage of nectars forming in wildflowers that blossom now in the high meadows because it is June, a time of year in the Rockies when—if we're lucky—thunderstorms take shape, passing rains sweep through afternoons and evenings, and the green world emerges. The moths seem to travel in groups; they rest in dark crevices and cracks, find openings in the back of a mailbox, or under doorframes, or lids of recycling carts. No one likes them but the swallows that swoop like crazy acrobats through intersections, catching moths mid-flight.

Meanwhile our human world of commerce and guns goes on in its mundane way: buying and selling, bullying and smashing, pulverizing, annihilating. This is known as creating markets—in other words, pumping up desires and hatreds so that the wasting of life becomes almost ordinary, shameless and thoughtless. But always something glitters or shines or sends up an aroma to distract us from grief and despair, to whet the appetite—fresh croissants and rich coffee, imported cheeses on a plate, ripe strawberries—clouds and mist tumbling off the flanks of the mountains, fog hovering over the flowing river.

The sky has turned pale orange, like the flesh of a not-quite-ripe cantaloupe. One red rose has opened in the garden, dark crimson. House Finches trill and chatter at the *pak, pak, pak* of a Flicker on a phone pole. No wind. Students in one massacre rushed the murderer and held him down till authorities took him into custody. An engineering student cradled the head of a young woman who had been wounded—blood on her chest—and when she cried out, "I'm dying," he tried using her cell phone to call numbers for "aunt" and "mommy," but neither answered.

Drift

Clouds form continents
overhead, a slow drift
that shifts maps of the world
over and over, countries
with no mass or weight,
borders without meaning,
rifts without malice.
I could lie here for hours
watching clouds come together
and tear apart, wind on my lips, my face.
I like the variations of light where
it touches the tops of mountains
as clouds disperse but persist,
causing sudden illuminations
at timberline, or a bright apprehension
of starlings circling in air.
I think a quick prayer,
not for me alone,
but for this place of rock
and water, fire and stone,
time of revelation and reverie—
for the consequences of our living,
and of having lived.

Waking in the Dark

For Marta Snow

Waking in the dark,
I lie in bed near the open window
and stare at the sky.

Stars pass by like migrants, each one
bent with a burden of light,
each murmuring a little song

remembered from childhood. The road
they tread is long, their feet dusty,
hardened by the persistence

and permanence of passage.
Night wind rushes past cool as velvet,
smelling faintly of lilac and sand.

It nudges the stars along,
and when they begin to wane
whispers encouragement,

explaining the necessity of movement,
proposing a purpose:
that simple relativity sustains us,

that the force of gratitude
connects us on our journey,
watchers of skies and stars.

Waking in the dark,
I lie in bed near the open window
and stare at the sky.

Notes

"Gacela," p. 2: The term was used by Federico García Lorca for his volume *El diván del tamarit,* which included both *gacelas* and *casidas.* The word seems to be related to the Arabic word *ghazal,* though Lorca does not observe the poetic "rules" that provide the structure for this form. I follow Lorca's lead in this.

"Maybeck houses," p. 2: Bernard Maybeck, an influential Berkeley architect in the early 20th-century, was known for his innovations in Arts and Crafts design. http://berkeleyheritage.com/berkeley_landmarks/maybeck_on_grove.html

"Steilacoom," p. 6: According to the Town of Steilacoom, Washington's website, "...the area had long been the home of the Steilacoom Tribe, roughly 600 people before [European] settlers arrived." http://www.townofsteilacoom.com/128/History

"Lavanda que te quiero lavanda," p. 31: I wrote this poem to help promote *Lavender Review,* an online publication of Lesbian poetry and art. The title was derived from the famous line "Verde que te quiero verde" found in Lorca's poem "Romance sonámbulo" from *Gypsy Ballads.*

"The Crags," p. 33: Weathered granite spires on the west slope of Pike's Peak, Colorado.

"Desde mi casita," p. 37: This and other "Santa Fe" poems were written while I was in residence at the School for Advanced Research in Santa Fe, New Mexico. The residency is offered to Native American poets. http://sarweb.org/index.php

"Cante jondo," p. 39: According to Lorca, in his essay on the subject, "The name *deep song* is given to a group of Andalusian songs whose genuine, perfect prototype is the Gypsy *siguiriya.* The *siguiriya* gave rise to other songs still sung by the people..." Probably incorrectly Lorca contrasts this older form of Gypsy song with the more contemporary style called *flamenco*. For more on this subject, see *Federico Garcia Lorca: In Search of Duende,* edited by Christopher Maurer.

"Siguiriya," p. 39: One of flamenco's oldest and deepest forms. According to the Studio Flamenco website, the word *siguiriyas* is "a corruption of the term *seguidillas,* a group of 18th Century songs and dances. *Siguiriyas* first emerged in Cádiz, Sevilla and Jerez de la Frontera. Slow, majestic and tragic, *Siguiriyas* is the most *jondo* of the *cante jondo* forms. Its lyrics focus on tragedy, inconsolable sorrow, and pain." http://www.studioflamenco.com/About_Siguiriyas.html

"Chimayó," p. 41: A village in New Mexico famous for its *Sanctuario* with its miraculous, healing dirt, and for its Hispanic arts, including weaving and woodcarving. A yearly pilgrimage is made to *El sanctuario de Chimayó* during Holy Week.

"Students in one massacre," p. 41: The line refers to a shooting at the University of Seattle in 2014. Please see http://www.seattletimes.com/seattle-news/1-dead-others-hurt-in-shooting-at-seattle-pacific-university-before-student-tackles-gunman/

About the Author

Janice Gould's tribal affiliation is Concow (koyoonk'auwi). She attended the University of California, earning a BA in Linguistics and a Master's in English, and later, from the University of New Mexico, a Ph.D. in English. A second Master's degree (in Library Science) was earned more recently at the University of Arizona. From 2014-16, Janice served as the Pike's Peak Poet Laureate, and was recognized by the city of Colorado Springs for her contribution to poetry with a "Spirit of the Springs" award. Her poetry has also garnered awards from the National Endowment for the Arts and the Astraea Foundation. Her latest book of poetry, *Doubters and Dreamers,* was a finalist for the Colorado Book and the Milton Kessler Book Awards. Her chapbook, *The Force of Gratitude,* was a finalist in the Charlotte Mew Poetry Chapbook contest. Janice is also author of *Earthquake Weather, Beneath My Heart, Alphabet,* and she co-edited a volume of essays on American Indian poetry, *Speak to Me Words.* She is an Associate Professor in the Women's and Ethnic Studies Program at the University of Colorado, Colorado Springs, where she teaches Native American Studies.

Acknowledgments

Some of the poems in this chapbook appeared (sometimes in slightly different form) in the following publications. Heartfelt thanks to the editors who accepted this work. Thanks, too, to many friends who offered encouragement and editorial advice.

Lavender Review: "Song" [originally titled "Steilacoom"], "Waking in the Dark"

Newsfocus, Women's Educational Society of Colorado College Newsletter: "Holy Wind"

Native Literatures: Generations: "Gacela of Bamboo and Plum Blossoms"

Pilgrimage Magazine: Story, Spirit, Witness, Place: "This Music"

Red Indian Road West: "Drift"

School for Advanced Research Annual Report: "Conditions for Poetry," "Gacela of Bamboo and Plum Blossoms"

Survivance, Sovereignty, and Story: Teaching American Indian Rhetorics: "Waking in the Dark," "Holy Wind"

The Almagre Review: La Revista Almagre: "Crazy Twenty-One," "Library," "Luhr's Lures," "Prodigal"

Three Coyotes: "Conditions for Poetry"

Understanding and Dismantling Privilege: "Holy Wind"

YouTube. "The Crags." https://youtu.be/riG5NyEdciM

YouTube. "Lavanda que te quiero lavanda." https://youtu.be/705y74CxJO8

Headmistress Press Books

Spine - Sarah Caulfield

Diatribe from the Library - Farrell Greenwald Brenner

Blind Girl Grunt - Constance Merritt

Acid and Tender - Jen Rouse

Beautiful Machinery - Wendy DeGroat

Odd Mercy - Gail Thomas

The Great Scissor Hunt - Jessica K. Hylton

A Bracelet of Honeybees - Lynn Strongin

Whirlwind @ Lesbos - Risa Denenberg

The Body's Alphabet - Ann Tweedy

First name Barbie last name Doll - Maureen Bocka

Heaven to Me - Abe Louise Young

Sticky - Carter Steinmann

Tiger Laughs When You Push - Ruth Lehrer

Night Ringing - Laura Foley

Paper Cranes - Dinah Dietrich

A Crown of Violets - Renée Vivien tr. Samantha Pious

On Loving a Saudi Girl - Carina Yun

The Burn Poems - Lynn Strongin

I Carry My Mother - Lesléa Newman

Distant Music - Joan Annsfire

The Awful Suicidal Swans - Flower Conroy

Joy Street - Laura Foley

Chiaroscuro Kisses - G.L. Morrison

The Lillian Trilogy - Mary Meriam

Lady of the Moon - Amy Lowell, Lillian Faderman, Mary Meriam

Irresistible Sonnets - ed. Mary Meriam

Lavender Review - ed. Mary Meriam

51935252R00034

Made in the USA
San Bernardino, CA
07 August 2017